Pilgrim Courage

Episodes from the Original Histo

OF PLIMOTH PLANTATIO

the journals o,

Pilgrim Courage

Pilgrim Courage

From a Firsthand Account

by WILLIAM BRADFORD

Governor of Plymouth Colony

Selected Episodes from His Original History

OF PLIMOTH PLANTATION

And Passages from the Journals of

William Bradford and Edward Winslow

Adapted and Edited

by E. BROOKS SMITH

ROBERT MEREDITH

and Illustrated

by Leonard Everett Fisher

Little, Brown and Company · Boston · Toronto

To our children, Jonathan Smith, Linda,
Susan, and Jane Meredith, and the
children of all Americans whose
forefathers came, early or late,
as pilgrims to a new land.

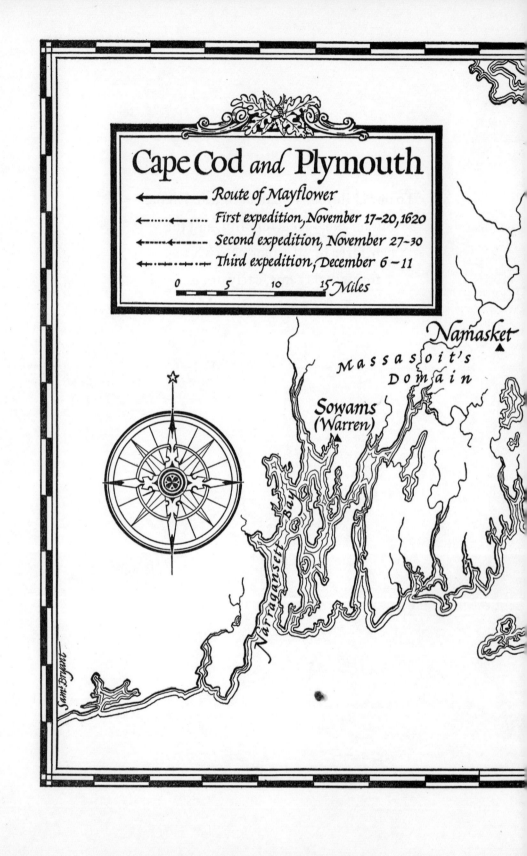

Cape Cod *and* Plymouth

← Route of Mayflower
←······←······ First expedition, November 17–20, 1620
←------←------ Second expedition, November 27–30
←·-·-←-·-·- Third expedition, December 6–11

0   5   10   15 Miles

Namasket ▲

M a s s a s o i t ' s
    D o m a i n

Sowams
(Warren) ▲

Narragansett Bay

Sam! Bryant

Clark's Island

Mayflower
anchored
November 11, 1620

Route of Mayflower

Patuxet
(Plymouth)
December
16

Billington's Sea

Shallop returns to Cape Harbor

Pamet
River

Landfall
a.m. Nov. 9

Cape Cod Bay

Route of shallop
and exploring party,
Third expedition, December 6

Nauset
(Eastham)

First encounter

Manomet

Manamoyick

Isle of Capawack
(Martha's Vineyard)

Prepared in co-operation with and approved by
Plimoth Plantation

Foreword

DURING the time of Queen Elizabeth I, the majority of the people of England and those who were in power believed that everyone should worship in the Established Church. But many others believed strongly that men could pray to God by themselves and worship Him simply, without ceremony or rule of bishops. Those men and women who broke away from the Established Church later became known as Separatists. They held secret meetings of worship though threatened with being put in prison.

In the year 1607, when this story begins, Queen Elizabeth had been dead four years and King James I ruled. At first he allowed the Separatists to speak their minds. Soon they bothered him so with their demands that he said unless they worshiped within the Church of England he would "harry them out of the land or else do worse."

In the north of England in the village of Scrooby a small group of Separatists banded together. They met secretly with their religious leaders and made plans to seek freedom of worship.

Among these people was a young man of strength and belief named William Bradford. Later, during the group's first year in America, he became their governor. Toward the end of his life he wrote a history of these strong-minded and sturdy people. He called them "Pilgrims" because they were wanderers in search of a land where they might establish a home more like the kingdom of heaven.

Contents

Pilgrim Courage

*Being Governor Bradford's
Firsthand Account of the
Escape, Voyage, Explorations
and Indian Encounters of the
First Settlers of Plymouth.*

Of Plymouth Plantation

A true story of the Pilgrims' adventures as told by their governor, William Bradford.

I shall try to tell their story in a plain style and with regard for the simple truth in all things, at least as near as I can judge.

CHAPTER I

Of Their Troubles, Persecutions, and Plans to Escape

WITH the work of some godly preachers many people became enlightened by the Word of God and began to reform their lives. When they began to live in the light of God's Word they were scoffed and scorned by the multitude. The ministers were told to follow the laws of the church or else be silent. And the poor people were sorely vexed by spying of church officers and actions of the courts. They were truly persecuted, yet they bore it with patience for many years.

But they could not long continue in this way. They were hunted and harried on every side, so that their former troubles were but as flea-bitings in comparison with those which were to come upon them.

Some were taken and clapped up in prison. Others had their houses beset and watched night and day. Most of them decided to flee, leaving their houses and means of livelihood. Seeing themselves thus molested and that there was no hope of staying, they decided by joint consent to go into Holland, where they heard was freedom of religion for all men. They also heard that some people from other parts of

England who had been persecuted for the same cause had gone to Amsterdam and other places in that country.

So they continued together about a year and kept their meetings every Sunday in one place or another, worshiping God among themselves. They decided to get over into Holland as best they could. This was in the year 1607.

To leave their native soil and country, their lands and livings, and all their friends was much. But to go into a country they knew not, where they must learn the language and find a new way of making a living, seemed a most desperate adventure and a misery worse than death. Also Holland was an expensive place to live and a country suffering the miseries of war. They had been used to plain country life and were not acquainted with the trades of the city. These things did not dismay them though they were sometimes troubled by them. Their desires were set on the ways of God and they believed in His providence.

CHAPTER II

Of Their Departure into Holland

A S IF this were not enough trouble, they were not even
allowed to leave England. The ports and harbors
were shut against them. They had to seek secret ways and
bribe the masters of the ships, paying very high rates for
their passage. Often times they were surprised and betrayed, and their belongings taken.

[They attempt escape and are discovered]

A large company of them planned passage from the town
of Boston. They had hired a ship wholly to themselves and
made agreement with the master to be ready on a certain
day. They were to go to a convenient place and wait in
readiness. After long waiting and large expenses, the master finally came and took them aboard in the night. But
when he had them and their goods aboard he betrayed
them, having plotted beforehand with the searching officers. The searchers took them, put them into open boats, and
there rifled and ransacked them. They were searched to
their shirts for money and even the women further than became modesty.

These officers then carried them back into town and made
them a spectacle before the people who came flocking on

all sides to behold them. Being stripped of their money, books, and much other goods, they were presented to the magistrates, who committed them to prison while messengers were sent to the Lords of the Council. Indeed the magistrates used them courteously and showed them what favor they could, but were unable to free them until orders came from the Council. After a month of imprisonment most of them were dismissed and sent back to their homes, but seven were still kept in prison and held for the higher courts.

[They make another attempt and an accident befalls them]

The next spring another attempt was made to get over to Holland from another harbor. It so happened that they met a Dutchman at Hull having a ship of his own. They made agreement with him and acquainted him with their condition, hoping to find more faithfulness in him than in the other ship's master. He told them not to fear, for he would do well by them. He was to take them aboard from a place between Grimsby and Hull, distant from any town. At the fixed time the women and children, with their goods, were sent to this place in a small boat hired for that purpose. The men were to meet them by land.

But it so happened that the women and children arrived a day before the ship came. As the sea was rough and the women became very sick, they asked the boatmen to put in to a creek near-by. The boat lay on the ground at low water. The next morning the ship came, but the small boat was fast aground and could not be stirred until about noon. In the meantime the ship's master, seeing how the matter was, sent his longboat to get the men aboard. He had seen that they were ready, walking about the shore.

But after the first boatful was got aboard and the seamen were ready to go for more, the master spied a great company of armed men. They were on horses and afoot, carrying halberds, muskets and other weapons. The people of the countryside had been roused to stop their departure and take them. The Dutch master, seeing what was happening, swore his country's oath *"Sacramente."* Having a fair wind, he weighed anchor, hoisted sails and away.

But the poor men who got aboard were in great distress about their wives and children. They watched them being taken away by the troops and were not able to help them. Those on the ship were themselves in distress, for they had only the clothes on their backs and scarcely a penny on them. Their goods had been left behind in the small boat. These troubles drew tears from their eyes, and they would have given anything to have been ashore again. Their wish was in vain, for there was no remedy. They must sadly part.

[Those at sea endure a fearful storm]

It was fourteen days before they reached Holland. During seven days of that time they saw neither sun, nor moon nor stars. They were driven near the coast of Norway. At one time the seas came over them so heavily that the seamen themselves gave up with shrieks and cries of despair. But when man's hope and help wholly failed, the Lord's power and mercy appeared. The ship rose again and gave the seamen courage to manage her.

I might declare with what fervent prayers and inner calm our company cried unto the Lord in this great distress. When water ran into mouths and ears, the seamen cried out, "We sink! We sink!" But our company with great faith cried, "Yet Lord Thou canst save!" The ship not only recovered, but the violence of the storm lessened. The Lord filled their troubled minds with comfort, and in the end brought them to their desired haven. The Dutch came flocking in wonder at their deliverance from so long and sore a storm.

[Those left behind weep and are miserable,
but a way is found]

The leaders of the group left behind made an escape before the troops in pursuit could take them. The others stayed by the women and assisted them. But it was pitiful to see these poor women in this distress. What weeping and crying on every side. Some cried for their husbands who were carried away in the ship. Others wept not knowing what should become of them and their little ones. Others again melted in tears seeing their poor little ones hanging about them, crying with fear and quaking with cold.

Being taken by the troops, they were hurried from one

place to another, and from one justice to another. In the end the magistrates knew not what to do with them. It was impossible to imprison so many women and innocent children. Nor could they be allowed to join their husbands against the law. They could not be sent home because they had no homes. Their houses had been sold. Much turmoil followed as they were sent around the countryside from one constable to another. Finally the courts set them free, and were glad to be rid of them.

All these poor souls endured many troubles and much misery in their wanderings on both land and sea. Those that saw them in public places were impressed by their godly bearing and Christian behavior. Although some gave up because of the hardships, others joined them with fresh courage. In the end they all got to Holland, some in one way and some in another. They met together again according to their desires with no small rejoicing.

CHAPTER III

Of Their Settling in Holland, the Manner of Their Living and Entertainment There

BEING now come into Holland they saw many goodly and fortified cities, strongly walled and guarded against the Spaniards with troops of armed men. Also they heard a strange language and saw the different manners of the people and their strange clothes. Everything differed greatly from the plain country villages where they grew up and had lived so long. It seemed as if they had come into another world. But they could not think about that too much, for they had other work to do and another kind of war to wage. Although they saw fair and beautiful cities flowing with all sorts of wealth and riches, they were poor people without proper work and place. Poverty came upon them like an armed man. They must fight it, for they could not fly from it. But they were armed with faith and patience. And though they were sometimes defeated, they won a victory by God's help.

They lived in Amsterdam about a year, but a disagreement arose with the English church already there. For this and some other reasons, they decided to move to Leyden, a fair and beautiful city. It was sweetly situated and made famous by its university. Since it was not a port like Amsterdam, they could not find as many means of living. But they found work to do and enjoyed the peace and spiritual comfort.

Being thus settled at Leyden, they continued many years in a comfortable condition. They enjoyed much sweet and delightful society under the able ministry and wise government of Mr. John Robinson, their minister, and Mr. William Brewster, who was made an elder of their church. They grew in knowledge and lived together in peace and love and holiness. Many others came to them from England, and they made a great congregation. And if any differences came between them or laws were broken, they were met and nipped in the bud. Those offenders that could not be cured were sent away. But this seldom came to pass, for they had mutual love and respect for one another.

[In Leyden their minister debates with the professors
of the university]

In these times there were great religious disputes in the
university. Mr. Robinson, their minister, even though he
taught them three times a week and wrote many books,
went constantly to hear the disputes at the university, on
one side as well as the other. He became so knowing of
the arguments of his belief and of the opponents' that
there was no one more fit to argue with them than himself. One of the professors and the chief preachers of the
city desired that Mr. Robinson dispute against the others.
Being a stranger in this country, he had no desire. But
the others persuaded him, saying that the truth would suffer
if he did not use his ability and nimbleness in argument. He
finally agreed and prepared himself against the time.
When the day came the Lord helped him to defend the truth
and to have the best of his opponent before the public au-
dience. He did this several times, and it made many praise
God that the truth had so famous a victory. He gained
honor and respect from the professors and from others who
loved the truth. So pleased were some of the influential
people in the city by him and his congregation that they
asked them to stay and come under the city's protection.

CHAPTER IV

Of the Reasons and Causes for Their Leaving Holland and Going to America

THEY lived in this city for eleven or twelve years, during the time when there was a truce between the Dutch and the Spaniards. Near the end of that time the elders and the wisest members of the congregation began to think about the coming dangers and look into the future for a remedy. They had grown older, some had been taken away by death, and all found living to be hard and the work not of their kind. They began to think about moving to some other place, not because of a giddy desire or newfangledness but for several weighty and solid reasons.

[They show reasons for leaving Holland]

First, they saw and found by experience that after a few years others who desired to be with them could not endure the hardness of the place. They preferred and chose the prisons in England to the liberty of Holland. Therefore it was thought best to find an easier place of living where they could practice their own trades. Then others would join them where they might have liberty and live comfortably.

Secondly, their leaders saw that although they bore these difficulties cheerfully and courageously, many were be-

coming old before their time and would sink under their burden. They had better move while they were still able.

Thirdly, because necessity was their taskmaster, they had to oppress their children with heavy labors. Although their children were willing, their bodies bowed under the weight and many became worn out in their early youth. But even worse, some of the children were drawn away from their parents, being tempted by evil examples set by the youth in the city. Some became soldiers, others ran away to sea. Others took even worse courses, further from the ways of their fathers.

Last and most important of all was their hope to lay some good foundation for the kingdom of Christ in remote parts of the world. They had a great desire to be the steppingstones for others to carry out so great a work.

[They argue about going to America]

They discussed the advantages and disadvantages of going to one of those vast and unpeopled countries of America. Although these countries were fit and fruitful to live in, they had no civilized people, only savage brutish men who ranged up and down like wild beasts.

Those who argued against moving to America complained that the long voyage would wear out the weak bodies of the women. They said that the miseries of the land would be too hard to be borne and that they would starve and become naked. The change of air, diet and drinking, they said, would infect their bodies with sore sicknesses and fatal diseases.

And if they should overcome these difficulties, then there was the continual danger of the savage people, who were cruel, barbarous and most treacherous in their rage and merciless when they captured. The savages were not only content to kill and take away life, but they delighted in tormenting men in the most bloody manner. They would skin alive some with the shells of fishes and cut off the arms and legs of others by piecemeal. Then they would broil these limbs on the hot coals and eat pieces of their flesh in their sight while they still lived. The very hearing of these things would move the very bowels of men to grate within them and make them weak and to quake and tremble. Those who argued against traveling to America further objected because of the great sums of money it would take to furnish such a voyage. They said that it was hard enough to live in a strange place like Holland, yet it was a neighbor country which was rich and civilized.

Those who desired to move to America argued that all great and honorable actions are always accompanied with great difficulties which must be overcome with courage. They said that many of the things which they feared might not even happen to them, and others by care might be prevented. All of these difficulties, they argued, might through the help of God with courage and patience be borne and overcome. If they remained in Holland with the truce over, the drum would beat again and the Spaniard might be as cruel as the savages of America. The starvation and pestilence might be as bad in Holland as across the seas.

After the arguments on both sides were heard, the majority decided to make plans and preparations for a voyage to America as best they could.

[They decide to plant their own colony in Virginia]

But where should they go in America? Some had thoughts about going to Guiana, or some of those fertile places in the hot climates. Others wanted to move to some part of Virginia where the English had already made a beginning. Those in favor of Guiana said that the country was rich, fruitful and blessed with a perpetual spring where vigorous nature brought forth all things in plenty without any great labor of man.

It was answered that although the country was fruitful and pleasant it was so hot that the people would get diseases because the climate would not agree with English bodies. Also the jealous Spaniard might not allow them to stay too long and would overthrow them as he had the French in Florida.

To live in Virginia would be comfortable, but they would then have to live among the English. Living under their government they would be in great danger of being persecuted again for the cause of religion. But if they lived too far away from the Virginia plantation, they would not be able to have their help or defense from the savages.

But finally they decided to live as a distinct body unto themselves, yet under the general government of Virginia. They planned to have friends ask the King if he would be pleased to grant them freedom of religion.

CHAPTER V

Of Their Preparations for This Weighty Voyage and Their Departure

TWO members were chosen and sent to England to discuss this plan, in 1617. They found that the Virginia Company desired very much that they should go to a distant part of Virginia, and they were willing to grant a patent. Some people in the Virginia Company thought that they could get the king's permission for freedom of religion and that this would be confirmed under the King's Great Seal.

But it proved to be a harder piece of work than they expected. The King said that he would not bother them if they behaved peaceably. But he also said that he would not put his great seal on a public document that gave them the right to freedom of religion. Although they were not pleased about the King's statement, they decided that a paper from the King, even if the seal were as broad as a house floor, would be worthless if the King ever changed his mind. Therefore they decided to get the best agreement that they could with both the government and the merchants in the Virginia Company. Many letters were sent back and forth between Holland and their spokesmen in England. But at last, after long dealings, they were granted a patent under the Virginia Company's seal. They would settle in the northern part of Virginia, near the Hudson River.

Since they had little money left from their hard life in Holland, they had to find money to pay for the voyage and settlement. After much difficulty they made an agreement with some London merchants which required that each person work for seven years, giving all his profits to the merchant company during that time in return for the money needed to start the plantation. At the end of seven years the houses, land, goods, and money would be divided fairly among the merchants and the settlers.

At length, after much writing and travel between Holland and England and after much debating, all things were got ready and provisions for the voyage were gathered. A small ship named *Speedwell* was bought and fitted in Holland. This ship was to carry some of them across the seas and stay with them in the new country for fishing and other uses that would help the colony. A larger ship was hired in London, named *Mayflower,* which would carry the rest of them to America and return to England with cargo.

[They depart from Holland and arrive in Southampton]

Being ready to depart, they held a day of fast and prayer. A company of friends went with them several miles to the harbor where the ship lay. So they left that pleasant city of Leyden, where they had lived for nearly twelve years. But they knew that they were pilgrims and looked not back, but lifted up their eyes to the heavens and their spirits were quieted.

When they arrived at the ship they found all things ready. Friends followed them even from Amsterdam to see them take ship and to say farewell. They had little sleep that night for they expressed their Christian love through friendly entertainment and talking.

On the next day, the wind being fair, they with their friends went aboard. This was a sad parting: what tears did gush from every eye, what sighs and sobs and prayers did sound amongst them. So mournful was this farewell that Dutch strangers standing on the dock could not refrain from tears. It was comfortable and sweet to see such true expression of love.

But the tide will not wait for any man and called them away that were so unwilling to part. Their reverend minister, Mr. Robinson, fell down upon his knees and all others with him. With watery cheeks they prayed to the Lord for his blessing. And then with mutual embraces and many tears they parted one from another. This would prove to be the last time that they would see most of these friends. The sails were hoisted.

With a prosperous wind they arrived at Southampton in a short time. The bigger ship from London, the *Mayflower,* was lying ready with all the rest of their company and some strangers who were to join them. After a joyful welcome and other friendly entertainments they decided to discuss their business arrangements and how best to carry out their expedition.

All things being now ready and every business completed, the company was called together. A letter from Mr. Robinson, their minister in Leyden, was read to them, wishing them happy success in this hopeful voyage. Then they divided themselves between the two ships. A governor and two or three assistants were chosen for keeping order and taking care of the provisions on each ship. The masters of the ships liked this arrangement. They set sail from Southampton about August 5, 1620.

CHAPTER VI

Of the Voyage to America and the Troubles That Befell Them

BEING thus put to sea, they had not gone far when the master of the smaller ship, *Speedwell,* complained that he found his ship so leaky that he dare not sail any farther until she be mended. He consulted with Mr. Jones, master of the *Mayflower,* and they decided to put in to Dartmouth to have the ship looked over and mended. This was done after a great loss of time. They were told by the workmen that they might proceed without fear or danger.

So with good hope, they put to sea again, thinking that they would go comfortably without further trouble. But it happened otherwise. Being about one hundred leagues beyond Land's End, the master of the *Speedwell* complained again. He said that his ship was so leaky that he must put it ashore or sink at sea, for they could scarcely keep her afloat with pumping. The masters of the two ships discussed the situation and decided to return to the coast. They put in to Plymouth.

No special leak was found, but the small ship was judged generally too weak for the voyage. Therefore it was decided to dismiss that ship and proceed with the *Mayflower* only. This caused great discouragement. They took out of the *Speedwell* all the provisions the *Mayflower* had room for. The leaders decided who should be sent back. Some were willing to stay behind, for they had become unhappy and fearful about the success of the voyage. Even so, it was a sad parting as one ship headed back for London and the other proceeded on her voyage. Like Gideon's army, this small number had been divided by God's providence, for He felt that even these few had been too many for the work that had to be done.

[How they pass the seas over]

These troubles blown over, and now all being together in one ship, they put to sea again with a prosperous wind. The wind continued several days and was some encouragement to them, even though many were seasick.

And I may not omit here a special work of providence. There was a proud and very profane young man, one of the seamen, of a lusty, able body, which made him the more haughty. He was always blaming the poor people for being sick and cursing them daily, and went so far as to tell them he hoped to help cast half of them overboard before they came to their journey's end and then to make merry with their goods. If anyone gently reproved him, he would swear most bitterly.

But it pleased God before they came half-seas over, to smite this young man with a painful disease, of which he died in a desperate manner, and so was himself the first thrown overboard and buried at sea. Thus his curses lit on his own head, and it was an astonishment to all his fellows, for they noted it to be the just hand of God upon him.

After they had enjoyed fair winds and weather for awhile, they encountered many cross-winds and met with many fierce storms. The ship was sharply shaken and her upper works made very leaky, and one of the main beams amidships was bowed and cracked. This put them in some fear that the ship would not be able to perform the voyage. So some of the leaders of the company, seeing the mariners feared the seaworthiness of the ship, as their mutterings showed, talked with the master and other officers about the danger. They debated whether to return rather than to cast themselves into such peril.

Truly, there was great confusion and difference of opinion among the mariners themselves. They wanted to do what they could to earn their wages (being now half the seas over). On the other hand, they did not want to risk their lives recklessly. But the master and others said they knew the ship to be strong and firm below water.

For the buckling of the main beam, there was a large iron jack the passengers brought out of Holland which would raise the beam into its place. If this were done, the carpenter and master said that with a post under it, set firm in the lower deck and made fast, it would do.

As for the decks and upper works, they would caulk them as well as they could. Though with the working of the ship the seams would open again, yet there would be no great danger if they did not set too much sail. So they gave themselves into the hands of God and decided to go on.

In several storms the winds were so fierce and the seas so high that they had to heave to and drift under very short sail for a number of days. As they lay to in one of the mightiest of the storms, a lusty young man called John Howland, venturing onto the open deck, was, with a sudden lurch of the ship, thrown into the sea. But it pleased God that he caught hold of the topsail halyards, which hung overboard and ran out at length. He held on, though he was some fathoms under water, till he was hauled up by the same

rope to the brim of the water. Then with a boat hook and other means he was got into the ship again. Though he was somewhat ill with it, he lived many years after and became a profitable member in both church and commonwealth.

In the whole voyage only one of the passengers died, a youth, William Butten, servant to Samuel Fuller.

[They arrive safely at Cape Cod]

After long beating at sea they fell with that land which is called Cape Cod. Checking the landfall and making sure of what it was, they were not a little joyful. After a meeting among themselves and with the master of the ship, they tacked about, resolved to stand for the southward, the wind and weather being fair, to find some place near Hudson's river for their settlement. But after they had sailed that course about half the day, they fell amongst dangerous shoals and roaring breakers. With the wind shrinking, they decided to go back to the Cape, happy to get out of those dangers before night overtook them. The next day they got into the Cape harbor where they rode in safety.

Being thus arrived in a good harbor and brought safe to land, they fell upon their knees and blessed the God of heaven, who had brought them over the vast and furious ocean, and had delivered them from all the perils and miseries thereof, again to set their feet on the firm and stable earth, their proper element.

[They make a compact]

Before the people came ashore they made a compact, the first foundation of their government in New England. They made this agreement because of the discontented and mutinous speeches from some of the strangers who had joined their company in London. The strangers said that when they came ashore they would do as they pleased, for nobody had power to command them. The patent was for Virginia, not New England. Another reason for making the compact was that such an act might be as firm as the Virginia patent, and in some ways more sure. The form of their compact was as follows:

In the name of God, Amen.

We whose names are underwritten, loyal subjects of our dread sovereign lord, King James, by Grace of God of Great Britain, France, and Ireland king, Defender of the Faith, and so forth, having undertaken, for the Glory of God and advancement of the Christian Faith, and honor of our King and Country, a voyage to plant the first colony in the northern parts of Virginia, do by this document solemnly and mutually in the presence of God, and one another, covenant and combine ourselves together into a civil body politic, for our better ordering and preservation and furtherance of the ends aforesaid; and by virtue of this document enact, constitute, and frame such just and equal laws, ordinances, acts, constitutions and offices, from time to time, as shall be thought right for the general good of the colony, unto which we promise all due submission and obedience. In witness we have hereunder subscribed our names at Cape Cod the eleventh of November, in the eighteenth year of the reign of our sovereign lord, King James.

1620 A.D.

After the compact was signed, they chose, or rather confirmed, Mr. John Carver their governor for the year. Later, as time would allow, they met and discussed laws and orders for their civil and military government as necessity required.

[They feel alone in the wilderness but are hopeful]

Here I cannot help making a pause and stand half amazed at this poor people's present condition. So I think the reader will too when he considers their state. Having passed over the vast ocean, and a sea of troubles in preparation for the voyage, they had now no friends to welcome them, nor inns to entertain or refresh their weather-beaten bodies, no houses, or much less towns, to go to, to seek help.

Scripture says that as a mercy to the Apostle Paul and his shipwrecked companions the barbarians showed no small kindness in refreshing them. But these savage barbarians were readier to fill their sides full of arrows than anything else. For the season, it was winter. Those who know New England winters know them to be sharp and violent, and subject to cruel and fierce storms. It is dangerous to travel to known places, much more to search an unknown coast.

Besides, what could they see but a frightening and lonely wilderness, full of wild beasts and wild men. What multitudes there might be of them, they knew not. Neither could they go, like Moses to the top of Mount Pisgah, to view from this wilderness a more goodly country to feed their hope as the Promised Land did. For wherever they turned their eyes (except upward to the heavens), they had little comfort from what they saw. Summer over, all things had a weather-beaten face. The whole country, full of woods and thickets, had a wild and savage look. If they looked behind them, there was the mighty ocean which they had passed. It now stood as a main bar and gulf to separate them from all the civilized parts of the world.

If it be said they had a ship to aid them, it is true. But what heard they daily from the master and crew? That they should take the shallop and with speed seek out a place to settle, not too far away. For the season was such that the master would not stir till a safe harbor was discovered by them where they wanted to be set ashore, which he might enter without danger. Also, the food supply was being all eaten up, but he must and would keep enough for the return trip. Some of the crew even muttered that if they did not get a place in time, they would put them and their goods ashore and leave them.

Think what weak hopes of supply and help they left behind to encourage them in these sad conditions and trials. Indeed, it is true that they had the love of their brethren in Leyden, but those left behind had little power to help, or even help themselves. The way things stood with the merchants at their coming away from England was not too promising. What could sustain them but the spirit of God and His grace?

May not and ought not the children of these fathers rightly to say, "Our fathers were Englishmen who came over this great ocean and were ready to perish in this wilderness, but they cried unto the Lord and He heard their voice and helped them in their adversity. Let them therefore praise the Lord, because He is good and His mercies endure forever."

CHAPTER VII

Of Their First Exploration

THUS arriving at Cape Cod on the eleventh of November, necessity (and the urging of the master and seamen) called them to look for a place to live. They had brought a large shallop with them from England, stowed in the ship. They now got her out and set their carpenters to work to trim her. Much bruised and shattered by the foul weather, she would be a long time mending.

A few men offered to go by land and explore the nearest places while the shallop was being worked on. One of the reasons they wanted to go was that as they came into the harbor, there seemed to be an opening some two or three leagues off to the south. The master thought it to be the mouth of a river. There might be danger in the attempt, but as they were determined, they were allowed to go.

[They see Indians and follow them]

Sixteen well-armed men were put under command of Captain Standish and given orders. They set out on the fifteenth of November. When they had marched about a mile by the seaside, they spied five or six men with a dog coming toward them. They were Indians! The savages fled from them up into the woods and whistled the dog after them. Captain Standish and his men followed, partly to see if they could speak with them and partly to find out if there might be more lying in ambush.

The Indians, seeing themselves followed, again left the woods and ran away on the sands as hard as they could. Captain Standish and his men could not come near them, but followed their tracks for several miles. Night coming on, they made camp, set out guards, and rested in quiet.

The next morning they followed the Indians' trail till it came to a great creek. They had to leave the sands and turn into the woods to get around the creek. They tried to follow the Indians now by guess, hoping to find their dwellings. But they soon lost both the Indians and themselves, and got into thickets that almost tore their clothes and armor in pieces. Yet they met no Indians nor found their houses. Nor could they find any water, which they greatly desired and stood in need of. Their only provisions were biscuits, Holland cheese, and a little bottle of brandy. These made them even more thirsty.

About ten o'clock they came into a deep valley full of brush, bayberry and long grass. They followed little tracks or paths and found springs of fresh water. They were heartily glad. They sat them down and drank their first New England water. In their great thirst, it tasted better than the best beer or finest wine.

When they had refreshed themselves, they went south in order to come to the other shore. They knew they were to cross over a neck of land. At length they got to the seaside and made a fire for the ship to see where they were, as they had been told to do. Then they marched toward the supposed river. Along the way they went into a valley, where they found a fine clear pond of fresh water about a musket shot broad and twice as long. Around it were many small

grapevines and signs of fowl and deer. They found sassafras growing there.

[They find a place where Indians had lived]

Shortly after, they came upon about fifty acres of clear
ground where the Indians had once planted corn. Some
thought it best, because they were so near the river, to go
down and travel on the beach. But walking in the sand made
several very tired and they lagged behind. They stopped
to gather them up and struck inland again.

They found a little path that led to some heaps of sand.
One was covered with old mats and a thing like a mortar
on top. An earthen pot lay in a little hole at the bottom of
the mortar. Wondering what it might be, they dug and
found a bow and some rotten arrows. They supposed there
were many other things, but because they thought them
graves, they put the bow back. Then everything was put
back the way it was, and the rest left untouched. The Indians
might not like their burial places to be ransacked.

Going on farther, they found new stubble, where corn
had been planted the same year. They passed many walnut
trees full of nuts and great stores of strawberry and grape
vines. Passing a few small fields, they found where a house
had lately been. Planks and a great kettle, a ship's kettle,
were still there. A heap of sand, made like the others but
newly done, lay hard by. Handprints showed, where it had
been paddled. Digging into it, they found a little old basket
full of fair Indian corn. Digging farther, they found a fine
great new basket, full of very fair corn. The corn was of
this year, six and thirty goodly ears, some yellow, some red,
and others mixed with blue. As they had seen none like it before, a goodly sight to see. The basket was round and small
at the top, handsome and cunningly made. Holding about

three or four bushels, it was as much as two of them could lift up from the ground.

[They take some corn and lose their way]

While they were doing this, they set most of the men on guard in a ring around them. They were in suspense what to do about the kettle. At length they decided, after much talk, to take the kettle and as much of the corn as they could carry. They would come back in the shallop. If they could find any of the Indians and come to parley with them, they would give them back the kettle and make a trade for the corn.

They took all the ears and put a good deal of the loose corn in the kettle for two men to carry away on a staff between them. Everybody put what he could in his pockets. The rest was buried again. They were so laden with armor they could carry no more.

Not far from this place they found the remainder of an old fort or palisade. They thought it had been made by other Christians. This was near the place they supposed a river to be. They went to it and found it was. The stream divided itself into two arms by a high bank where it poured into the sea. The closer arm was the lesser. The other was twice as big and seemed likely to be a harbor for ships. Whether it was fresh water or only an inlet from the sea, they had no time to find out as they had orders to be out only two days. A canoe was on each side of the stream. Lest there be fear for their safety, they started back to the ship.

That night they came back again to the fresh water pond, and made their camp. They made a great fire and a windbreak to keep them warm. A good guard was kept with three sentinels at all times. Everyone stood watch when his time came. The watch was timed by the burning of five or six inches of the match kept lit for firing the muskets. It was a rainy night.

In the morning they took the kettle and sunk it in the pond and put their muskets in firing trim, for none of them would go off because of the wet. They skirted the woods to come home, but soon became puzzled and lost their way. As they wandered they came to a tree where a limb was bent down over a bow and some acorns spread underneath. Stephen Hopkins said it was to catch a deer. William Bradford, in the rear, came up to look. As he went about it, the limb gave a sudden jerk up, and he was caught by the leg. It was a very pretty device, made with a rope of the Indians' making. The noose was as artfully made as any roper in England could make. They brought it back with them.

In the end they got out of the woods, about a mile from the head of the creek. They saw three bucks there, but would rather have had one than see three. They stirred up three pair of partridge, and as they came along the creek, saw great flocks of wild geese and ducks. The geese and ducks were very fearful of them and very flighty. They marched some while in the woods and some while on the sands, and other while in the water up to the knees. At length they came near the ship. They shot off their pieces for a signal and the longboat came to fetch them.

Like the men Moses sent to spy out the land of Canaan, they brought with them fruits of the country and showed their brethren. The corn and their safe return made the people marvelously glad, and their hearts encouraged.

CHAPTER VIII

Of Their Second Exploration

WHEN the shallop was fit (indeed before she was fully fitted, for they later did two days of work on her), twenty-four men were named to go and make a full exploration of the river. Master Jones wanted to go with them, and he took such of his sailors as he thought would be most useful, making thirty-four men in all.

Master Jones was made leader in recognition of his kindness and eagerness to be helpful. They set forth on Monday, the twenty-seventh of November. The weather proved rough, with cross-winds, and they were forced, some in the shallop, some in the longboat, to row to the nearest shore they could get to in the wind and wade ashore in water up to their knees.

The wind blew so strong the shallop was forced to harbor there for the night. The land party, that had come ashore in the longboat, arranged to have the shallop meet them when it could, and marched six or seven miles farther. It blew and snowed all that day and night. Some of the people who died later caught their first sickness here.

The next day the shallop joined them about eleven o'clock, and they all got aboard. The wind being good, they sailed to the river they had discovered before, which they named Cold Harbor. They found it not navigable for ships, only for boats. They landed between the two creeks and marched some four or five miles by the larger of them, the shallop following.

Night grew on. The men were tired with marching up and down the steep hills and deep valleys, which lay half a foot thick with snow. Master Jones, wearied with marching, said they should make camp, although some of them would have marched further. So they made camp for the night under a few pine trees. They shot three fat geese and six ducks for supper; they ate with the stomachs of hungry soldiers, for they had eaten little all that day. They decided that on the next day they would go up to the head of the river, supposing it would prove to be fresh water.

But in the morning they decided the land was too hilly to settle on and the harbor not big enough. So they turned to the smaller creek that they might go over and look for the rest of the corn that they had left behind. When they came to the creek, there was a canoe, on dry ground. A flock of geese was in the river, so one man made a shot and killed a couple of them. They launched the canoe to get the geese, and then used it to get across the creek, seven or eight men at a time.

They marched to the place where the corn had been found, which they called Cornhill. They dug and found the rest, of which they were very glad. They dug in another place and found a bottle of oil. In another place they dug up two or three basketfuls of corn and a bag of beans of various colors. Still more corn was found, until there were ten bushels in all. They had enough to use for seed.

Surely it was God's good providence that they found the corn. Otherwise they could not have managed. They did not know how to find or meet the Indians, unless the Indians attacked them. And if they had not made the first exploration trip they would never have seen a grain of it, in all likelihood, for the ground was now frozen hard. They had to hack and carve with cutlasses and short swords to get down a foot and then pry the corn out with levers. They had forgotten to bring their tools.

Foul weather coming up, Master Jones wanted to go back to the *Mayflower,* but some of the men wanted to make further discovery and find out where the Indian houses were. They sent back the weakest and those who were sick, as well as all the corn. Eighteen men stayed and spent the night. They desired the shallop to return next day and bring some mattocks and spades.

[They march into the woods and find
more Indian graves]

The next morning they followed certain beaten paths of the Indians into the woods, supposing they would lead to some town or houses. After a while they came upon a very broad beaten path almost two feet wide. They lighted all their matches to be ready to fire their matchlock muskets as they thought they were near the Indians' dwellings. But in the end they found it was a path made to drive deer in when hunting, as they supposed.

When they had marched five or six miles into the woods and could find no signs of any people, they turned another way. Coming into open ground, they found a place like a grave, but it was much bigger and longer than any they had yet seen. It was also covered with boards. They wondered what it might be, and decided to dig it up.

First they found a mat, and under that a fair bow. Under that, another mat, and then a board about three-quarters of a yard long, finely carved and painted, with three tines or prongs on top like a crown. Between the mats were bowls, trays, dishes, and such trinkets. At length they came to a fair new mat, and under that, two bundles, one larger than the other. They opened the greater and found in it a great quantity of fine red powder and the bones and skull of a man. The skull had fine yellow hair still on it. Bound up with it was a knife, a packing needle, and two or three old iron things. The bundle was made of a sailor's blouse and a pair of cloth breeches. The red powder was a kind of embalming powder.

They opened the lesser bundle also and found the skeleton of a little child with strings and bracelets of fine white beads about it. There was also a child's bow. They covered the corpses again.

There was a variety of opinions about the embalmed man. Some thought he was an Indian lord or king. Others said the Indians all had black hair and one was never seen with brown or yellow hair. Some thought him a Christian of special note who had died amongst them, and the Indians had buried him to honor him. Others thought the Indians had killed him and buried him this way to triumph over him.

[They find some Indian dwellings]

While they were ranging around and searching, two of the sailors, who had just come ashore from the shallop, by chance saw two houses. They had lately been lived in, but the people were now gone. Having their pieces with them and hearing nobody about, the sailors entered the houses and took out some things, but did not dare to stay around. They came to join the others. Seven or eight went back with them and found they had passed within an arrow's flight of the place without seeing it.

The houses were made with long young sapling trees, bent with both ends stuck in the ground. They were made round like an arbor, and covered down to the ground with thick, well-made mats. The door was not over a yard high, made of a mat that could be pulled aside. The chimney was a wide open hole in the top, for which they had a mat, to cover it close when they pleased. One might stand and walk upright in the house. In the middle were four stakes driven into the ground with small sticks across them to hang their pots over the fire. Around the fire they had mats for beds. The houses were double matted, with the newer and better mats covering the inside.

In the houses they found wooden bowls, trays and dishes. There were earthen pots, hand baskets made of crab shells worked together, and an English pail or bucket without a handle. There were also baskets of several sorts, large and small, fine and coarse. Some were curiously made, with black and white interwoven in patterns. They found two or three deer's heads, one newly killed. A number of deer's feet were stuck up in the houses, as well as harts' horns, eagles' claws, and things of that sort. There were two or three baskets full of parched acorns, pieces of fish, and a piece of broiled herring. They found also a little silk grass and to-bacco seed, with some other seed they did not know.

Outside were several bundles of sedge, bulrushes, and other stuff for making mats. Thrust into a hollow tree were two or three pieces of venison, but only fit for dogs to eat. They took some of the best things and left the houses standing as they were.

As it was growing toward night and the tide almost out, they hurried down to the shallop and got aboard the ship that night. They meant to bring some beads and other things to leave in the houses as a sign of peace and that they wanted to trade. But they could not do it because of their hasty departure from Cape Cod. They meant to pay in full for what they took when they should meet with any of the Indians (as they did about six months later, to the Indians' satisfaction).

While some were employed in this exploration, it pleased God that Mistress White gave birth to a son. He was called Peregrine, which means pilgrim.

[They discuss settling on Cape Cod]

Having explored the area around Cornhill, they debated settling there. Some thought it best, for the following reasons:

First, there was a convenient harbor for boats if not for ships.

Secondly, good corn ground was ready at hand. They knew it was productive from the corn they had found. The seed would grow better on its native ground.

Thirdly, Cape Cod was likely to be a place of good fishing. They saw daily great whales, of the best kind for oil and bone. The whales came close to the ship, and in fair weather, swam and played about. Once when the sun shone warm, one came and lay above water within half a musket shot of the ship. Two men prepared to shoot to see whether it would stir or not. But only one fired. His musket blew up in his hands, lock, stock, and barrel, yet thanks be to God, neither he nor anyone else was hurt, although many were standing about. The whale saw its chance, gave a snuff, and away!

Fourthly, the place was likely to be healthful, secure, and defensible.

But the last and special reason was that now the heart of winter and unseasonable weather had come. They could not go along the coast exploring without danger of losing men and boats. The variable winds and sudden storms might mean the death of them all. Cold and wet lodging had given most of the people bad coughs, and if they stayed on the ship much longer their lives would be endangered. There was some beer, butter, meat, and other such food left which would quickly be gone. Then they would have nothing to keep them strong during the hard work of getting settled ashore. And as long as there was enough food the ship would stay. When that grew low, the ship would leave and let them get by as best they could.

Others urged greatly going to Agawam, a place twenty leagues off to the north. First, they had heard it to be an excellent harbor for ships with better ground for crops and better fishing.

Secondly, for anything they knew, there might be close-by a far better place. It would be a great bother to have to move after getting settled.

Thirdly, the water was only in ponds on the Cape, and it was thought there would be none in summer.

Fourthly, the water would have to be carried up a steep hill.

It was finally decided to explore the bay, but in no case so far as Agawam. Robert Coppin, the pilot, told of a great navigable river and good harbor in the other headland of the bay, almost opposite Cape Cod, not more than eight leagues in a straight line. He had been there once, and because one of the wild men with whom they had been trading stole a harpoon, they called it Thievish Harbor.

[Another kind of danger is narrowly escaped]

On Tuesday the fifth of December they escaped a great danger growing out of the foolishness of a boy, Francis

Billington. In his father's absence he got gunpowder and shot off a musket or two. He made some squibs with the gunpowder and exploded them. He took up a loaded fowling piece in a cabin full of people and shot it off. A little barrel of powder was open and scattered about, as well as flint and pieces of iron. By God's mercy the powder was not set off and no harm was done.

CHAPTER IX

Of the Third Exploration and First
Encounter with the Indians

A COMPANY of volunteers was selected to go on a third trip of exploration. December fifth was too foul to venture forth, but on the sixth they set out, though the day was almost over before they got everything ready. The company was made up of Captain Standish, Master Carver, William Bradford, Edward Winslow, John Tilley, Edward Tilley, John Howland, and three of the men from London, Richard Warren, Stephen Hopkins, and Edward Dotey. Two of the seamen who were to stay with the plantation and help with fishing, John Allerton and Thomas English, went. From the ship's company were two of the master's mates, Master Clarke and Master Coppin, the master gunner and three sailors. They set out in the shallop to go around the deep bay of Cape Cod with orders not to go north of the harbor Master Coppin spoke of.

The weather was very cold, and it froze so hard that the spray of the sea lighting on the men's coats made them look glazed. Yet that night they got down to the bottom of the bay in good time. As they drew near the shore, they saw ten or twelve Indians very busy about something. They landed a league or two from them, and had a hard time putting ashore because of the shallows. Being landed, it grew late, and they made themselves a barricade with logs and boughs as well as they could in the time they had. Setting out a sentinel, they lay down to rest. The smoke of the savages' fire could be seen.

When morning came they divided their company, some to go along the shore in the boat, the rest to march through the woods to see the land and if any place might be fit for them to live in. They came also to the place where the Indians were the night before. They had been cutting up a great fish like a grampus, having fat two inches thick like a hog. Some pieces had been left near-by. Those in the shallop found two more of the fish dead on the sands, a thing usual after storms in that place because of the great sand flats that lie off the shore. So they ranged up and down all that day, but found no people nor any place they liked.

When the sun grew low, they hastened out of the woods to meet the men in the shallop, to whom they made signs to come to them in a creek close by. They did at high water and they were very glad, for they had not seen each other all day, since the morning. So they made a barricade with logs, stakes, and thick pine boughs, to the height of a man, leaving it open to leeward. Thus they had a shelter from the cold and the wind (making their fire in the middle and lying around it) and a defense from any sudden assaults of the savages, if they should surround them. So being very weary, they went to sleep.

About midnight, they heard a hideous and great cry and their sentinel cried, "Arm! Arm!" They quickly got up and fired a couple of muskets, and the noise stopped. They decided it was a pack of wolves or other wild beasts, for one of the seamen told them he had often heard such a noise in Newfoundland.

They rested till about five o'clock in the morning. The tide and their plan to leave made them stir early. After prayer they prepared for breakfast, and day dawning, it was thought best to be carrying things down to the boat. Some said it was not best to carry the arms down. Others said they would be the readier for they had folded them up in their coats from the dew. Three or four would not carry theirs till they went themselves. Yet as it happened, the water not being high enough, they laid their arms down on the bankside and came up to breakfast.

Presently, all of a sudden, they heard a great and strange cry, which they knew to be the same voices they heard in the night, though the notes varied. One of the company, being out, came running in crying, "Men! Indians! Indians!" At that, arrows came flying amongst them.

The men ran with all speed to get their muskets from the bank, as by the good providence of God they did. In the meantime, of those that were there ready, two pieces were fired. Two more stood ready in the entrance of their barricade, but were commanded not to shoot till they could take full aim. The other two loaded their pieces as fast as they could, for there were only four men who had arms there to defend against the first attack.

The cry of the Indians was dreadful, especially when they saw the defenders run out toward the shallop to recover their arms. The Indians cried, "Woak, woak ha ha hak woak," and wheeled about upon them. But some running out with coats of mail on and cutlasses in their hands, soon got their arms and let fly amongst the Indians, quickly stopping their violence. Yet there was a lusty and valiant savage who stood behind a tree well within musket range and let his arrows fly. He was seen to shoot three arrows, which were all avoided. He stood three musket shots,

till someone, taking careful aim at him, made the bark or splinters of the tree fly about his ears, after which he gave an extraordinary shriek and away went all of them.

Leaving some to keep the shallop, the men came out and chased the Indians about a quarter of a mile, shouted once or twice, shot off two or three of their pieces and returned. This they did so the Indians might know that they were not afraid of them or discouraged in any way.

Thus it pleased God to vanquish their enemies, and give them deliverance, and by His special providence keep anyone from being hurt or hit, though arrows came close by on every side, and several of their coats hanging in their barricade were shot through and through. Afterward they gave God solemn thanks and praise for their deliverance, gathered up a bundle of the Indian arrows, which they sent to England later by the master of the ship, and called that fight the first encounter.

CHAPTER X

Of Their Happening on Plymouth Harbor

FROM the place of the first encounter they continued along the coast in the shallop, but found no likely harbor. They hurried to a place that their pilot (Mr. Coppin, who had been in the country before) assured them was a good harbor. He said he had been in it and they could reach it before night. They were glad, for the weather turned foul. After some hours sailing, it began to snow and rain. About the middle of the afternoon the wind increased and the sea grew rough. Their rudder broke and it was all two men could do to steer her with a couple of oars.

Their pilot bid them be of good cheer, for he saw the harbor. The storm increasing and night drawing on, they put up what sail they could to get in while they could see. But at this, their mast broke in three pieces and their sail fell overboard in the raging sea. They were almost lost, yet by God's mercy they recovered themselves, and having the tide with them, came into the harbor.

But the pilot said he was deceived about the place. The Lord be merciful unto them, for his eyes never saw it before. He and the mate would have run her ashore, in a cove full of breakers, before the wind. But a lusty seaman who steered told those who rowed, if they were men, about with her, or they would be cast into the sea. So they brought her about with speed. He bid them be of good cheer and row lustily, for there was a fair sound before them. He doubted not but they should find one place or another where they might ride in safety. And though it was very dark and rained sore, yet in the end they got under the lee of a small island and remained there all night in safety.

They did not know it was an island till morning. They were divided in their minds. Some would stay on the boat for fear they might be amongst the Indians. Others were so weak and cold, they could not bear it, and went ashore. With much ado (all things being so wet), they made a fire. The rest were glad to join them, for after midnight the wind shifted to the northwest and it froze hard.

Though this had been a day and night of much trouble and danger unto them, yet God gave them a morning of comfort and refreshment (as He usually does to His children). The next day was a fair and sunshining day, and they found themselves to be on an island secure from the Indians. They could dry their stuff, fix their pieces, and rest themselves. They gave God thanks for His deliverance. And this being the last day of the week, they prepared to keep the Sabbath.

[They explore around the harbor,
fetch the *Mayflower*, and make a landing]

On Monday they sounded the harbor and found it deep enough for shipping. They marched also into the land and found several cornfields and a little running brook. A very good place to settle, they supposed. They returned to the ship with good news, which much comforted their hearts.

On the fifteenth of December, they weighed anchor to go to the place they had discovered. They came within two

leagues of it, but could not get there. On the sixteenth the wind came fair and the *Mayflower* sailed safe into harbor.

The harbor was greater than Cape Harbor, compassed with goodly land, and in the bay were two fine islands. The islands were uninhabited and covered with woods: oak, pine, walnut, and beech. The bay seemed a most hopeful place, with innumerable store of fowl, and fish in season, such as skate, cod, flounder, and herring. Abundance of mussels, crabs, and lobsters was found there. The harbor was fashioned like a sickle or fishhook.

On the eighteenth they went along the coast in the woods some seven or eight miles, but saw not an Indian or Indian house. They saw only where Indians had once lived and planted their corn. They found no navigable rivers, but four or five brooks of fresh water that all ran into the sea. The soil was a black mold and deep. They saw great oaks, pines, walnut, beech, ash, birch, hazel, holly, aspen, sassafras, and grapevines. They saw cherry trees, plum trees, and many kinds they did not know. Many kinds of herbs they found in winter: strawberry leaves, sorrel, yarrow, liverwort, water cress, great stores of leeks and onions, excellent flax and hemp. There was sand, gravel, and excellent clay, no better in the world. The clay was good for making pots and washed like soap. There was great store of stone, though somewhat soft. The brooks at this time were beginning to fill up with fish. That night, many weary with marching, they went aboard ship.

The nineteenth of December, after landing and viewing the places as well as they could, they concluded by a majority of voices to settle on the mainland. They chose the high ground where there was a great deal of cleared land that had been planted with corn three or four years before, where a very sweet brook ran under a hill and many fine springs were. They could harbor their boats and shallops there very well and there would be good fish in the brook. In one field was a great hill on which they meant to build a platform and put their cannon, to command the area all about. From thence they could see into the bay, far out to sea, and across to Cape Cod.

CHAPTER XI

Of Their Building and the Troubles That Befell Them During the First Winter

ON SATURDAY, the twenty-third, as many as could went ashore to fell and carry timber for building. Monday, the twenty-fifth, they went on shore to work, so no man rested on Christmas Day. But on board ship that night the master of the ship gave out beer.

They took note how many families there were and asked all single men to join with some family. This was in order to build fewer houses, making nineteen households. The larger families got larger plots. For every person the plot would be eight feet wide and fifty feet long. Then plots were staked out.

These plots were thought big enough at the first for a house and garden with a fence around. The people were weak and ill and could scarcely do more. The explorations and wading at Cape Cod had brought much weakness, and afterward many deaths.

Friday and Saturday they got ready to work, but the weather was stormy and cold, and very wet. About six or seven miles away smoke rose from Indian fires. On Thursday, the fourth of January, Captain Miles Standish with four or five men went to see if they could meet with any of the Indians where the smoke had risen. They saw some empty houses, but no Indians. As they came home they shot an eagle. It made excellent meat, tasting just like mutton.

Monday, the eighth of January, was a very fair day and fine for working. Master Jones sent the shallop fishing. Although they were in danger from a storm at sea, they brought home three large seals and an excellent cod. The cod gave promise of good fishing later.

This same day Francis Billington, the boy who almost blew up the *Mayflower,* went exploring with one of the ship's mates. The week before he had climbed a tree on top of a hill and said he saw a great sea. They went three miles and found no sea but two lakes from which their town brook came. The larger lake was about five or six miles around with a small island in it. They were afraid when they saw seven or eight Indian houses, being only two with one musket, but the Indians had not lived there lately. Afterward the lakes were called Billington's Sea.

Tuesday, the ninth of January, was a reasonably fair day. They went to work at building a town, in two rows of houses for more safety. Every man was to build his own house. It was thought each would work with more haste than working in common. But the common house and gathering place had to be finished first as all who were ashore slept in it. They made it about twenty feet square. All it lacked was a roof. Some made mortar, some gathered thatch, but foul weather hindered them much. At this time of the year they could only work half the week.

[Two of their number wander off and
become lost in the woods]

On the twelfth, John Goodman and Peter Brown at dinner time took their food in their hands and went for a walk.

Going a little off, they found a small lake with the help of a mastiff bitch and a spaniel. By the water they found a deer. The dogs gave chase. The men followed until they lost themselves. They wandered all that afternoon and got very wet. At night it froze and began to snow. They were lightly dressed and had no weapons, except their sickles, nor any food. They ranged up and down, but could find no Indian huts. They were much troubled, finding neither shelter nor food. In frost and snow they were forced to make the earth their bed and the elements their covering.

They were terrified in the night. They thought they heard two lions, not knowing what beasts might be in this land. Then they heard a third, sounding very near. Not knowing what to do, they resolved to climb up a tree as the safest refuge, cold as it might be up there. They stood at the tree's roots in order to climb up quickly. They were going to hold the mastiff bitch in the tree, for they thought the lion sure to get her. But it pleased God that the beasts came not. They spent the night walking up and down under the tree.

Soon as it was light, they traveled again, passing many ponds and brooks and woods, and in one place, where the Indians had burned over a space five miles in length, fine open country. In the afternoon, from a high hill, they saw the two islands in the bay. That night they got back, ready to faint with travel and want of food, and almost frozen. John Goodman had to have the shoes cut off his feet, they were so swollen. It was a long time before he could walk without limping.

But a little over a week later John Goodman went out to use his lame feet, taking the little spaniel with him. A little way from the plantation two great wolves ran after the dog. The dog ran between his legs for protection. John Good-man had nothing in his hand, but picked up a stick and threw at one of the wolves. He hit him and they both ran away, but they came back. He picked up a stake, and the wolves sat back on their tails, grinning at him a good while. Then they went their way.

[They are beset by fire, disease, and death]

The common house caught fire from time to time from sparks coming out of the chimney and flying into the thatch, which burned up instantly. But the roof remained, little hurt. All they had to do was put on more thatch. Once there was danger to Mr. Carver and William Bradford when both lay sick abed. If they had not risen with good speed, they would have been blown up by gunpowder stored under the beds. The common house was full of beds and loaded muskets. Through God's mercy they had no harm.

In these hard and difficult beginnings they found discontent and murmurings in some, and mutinous speeches and bearing in others. But these troubles were soon overcome by the wisdom, patience, and just and equal running of things by the Governor and the majority, who worked together in the spirit of the compact made on the *Mayflower*.

In two or three months' time half of their company died, especially in January and February. In the depth of winter, lacking houses and other comforts, sick with scurvy and other diseases that the long voyage and crowding had brought on them, sometimes two or three died in one day. Of one hundred people, scarce fifty remained.

Of the fifty, in the time of most distress, only six or seven were sound. These six or seven, to their great commendation be it said, spared no pains, night nor day. With abundance of toil and hazard of their own health, they got wood, made fires, cooked food, made beds, washed filthy clothes, dressed and undressed the sick. In a word, they did all the homely and necessary tasks for them that dainty and queasy stomachs cannot bear to hear named. All this was done willingly and cheerfully, without any grudging in the least, showing their true love unto their friends and brethren. A rare example and worth remembering.

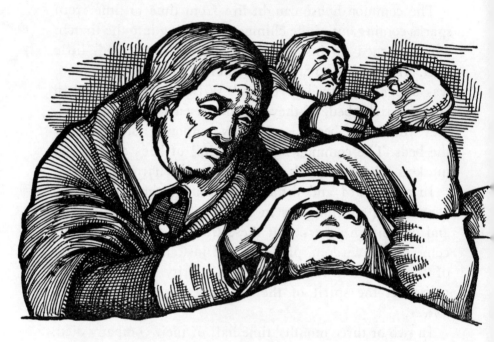

Two of these seven were Mr. William Brewster, the reverend Elder, and Miles Standish, their captain and military commander. I and many others owed much to them in our low and sick condition. The Lord so upheld these persons that in this general calamity they were not at all infected either with sickness or lameness. What I have said of these, I may say of many others who died in the general sickness, and others yet living, that while they had breath, or any strength left, they helped all having need of them. I doubt not but their reward is with the Lord.

I must tell another remarkable story not to be forgotten. This calamity fell among the passengers who had been hurried ashore and made to drink water so the seamen might have more beer. One man [Bradford himself], in his sickness wanting but a small cup of the nourishing beer, was told by the ship's master, "If you were my own father, you should have none." But the disease began to fall amongst the seamen also, so that almost half of their company died before they left for England. They lost many of their officers and lustiest men, such as the boatswain, the gunner, three quartermasters, the cook, and others. The master of the ship was stricken in his heart by this and sent word to the Governor that he should send for beer for those ashore who needed it, though he had to drink water homeward bound.

Amongst the ship's company there was a far different kind of conduct in this misery than amongst the passengers. Those that before had been boon companions in drinking and jollity in the time of their health and welfare, began to desert one another in this calamity. They said they would not hazard their lives. They would be infected by coming to help the sick in their cabins. So, after they lay helpless, they would do little or nothing for them. If they were dying, let them die.

The passengers still aboard showed what mercy they could, making some of the seamen relent in the hardness of their hearts. The boatswain, who was a proud young man, would often curse and scoff at the passengers. When he grew weak, they had compassion on him and helped him. Then he confessed he did not deserve it at their hands; he had abused them in word and deed. "Oh!" says he. "You, I now see, show your love like Christians to one another, but we let one another lie and die like dogs."

One seaman lay cursing his wife, saying if it had not been for her he would never have come on this unlucky voyage. Then he cursed his fellows, saying he had done this and that for some of them, spent such and such a sum amongst them. But now they were weary of him and did not help him in his need.

Another promised his companion all he had if he died in return for help in his weakness. The companion went and got a little food and made him a meal once or twice. But as he did not die as soon as expected, the companion went amongst his fellows and swore the rogue wanted to cheat him. He would see him choked before he made him another meal. Yet the poor fellow died before morning.

Spring now approaching, it pleased God the deaths stopped and the sick and lame got quickly better, putting new life into all. Though they had borne their sad afflictions with as much patience as any people could, it was the Lord who upheld them, and had prepared them beforehand, many having been under His firm rule from their youth.

Saturday, the third of March, the wind was south and the morning misty. Toward noon the day turned warm and fair. The birds sang in the woods most pleasantly. At one o'clock it thundered, the first they had heard in this country. It was strong, with great claps, but short. After an hour it began to rain and rained steady till midnight.

CHAPTER XII

Of Their Friendly Relations with the Indians

ALL this while the Indians came skulking about. Sometimes they showed themselves at a distance, but ran away when approached. Once the Indians stole some tools where Miles Standish and Francis Cooke had been at work and were gone to dinner.

But on Friday the sixteenth there was cause for alarm. A savage came boldly all alone, walked past the houses, and straight to the meeting house. He would have walked in had he not been stopped at the door. He saluted them in English and bid them welcome. He had learned some broken English amongst the men who came to fish on the coast to the northeast. He knew by name most of the captains, commanders, and masters who came there. The Indian's name was Samoset.

[They talk with Samoset and he tells them of this place before they came]

Samoset was a man free in speech, so far as he could express his mind, and of good bearing. As he was the first savage they could talk to, they questioned him about many things. He said he was not of these parts, but of the northeast coast, and one of the sagamores or lords there. He had been in these parts eight months. His home lay a day's sail away with a great wind or five days by land. He spoke of the whole country, the provinces, their sagamores, their number of men and strength. The wind beginning to rise a little, they cast a horseman's coat about him, for he was stark naked except for a little bit of leather about his waist.

Samoset had a bow and two arrows. He was a tall, straight man. The hair of his head was black, long behind and short in front, but he had no hair at all on his face. He asked for beer, but he was given brandy and biscuit, butter and cheese, pudding and a piece of mallard. He liked it all well, and knew such things from being amongst the English.

He told them this place was called Patuxet, and that about four years before all the Indians who lived here died of the plague. So there would be none to hinder their possession of the place. He said there was one man left named Squanto, who had been in England and spoke better English than he.

They spent the afternoon talking with him. They would have been glad to get rid of him for the night, but he was not willing to go. They thought to put him on shipboard for safety and went into the shallop, but the wind was high and the water low, so they had to turn back. At last he was lodged for the night at Stephen Hopkins's house, with a watch over him.

They dismissed him on Saturday in the morning with the present of a knife, a bracelet and a ring. He promised to come again within a night or two, and to bring with him some neighboring Indians and such beaver skins as they had to trade.

On Sunday Samoset came again with five other tall savages. Every man had a deer's skin on him, and the main

one had a wildcat's skin on one arm. Most of them had tight-fitting deerskin leggings up to their hips, and above these up to the waist another piece of leather. They looked as if they were wearing Irish trousers. Their complexion was like that of the English Gypsies. They had very little hair on their faces and that on their heads hung down to the shoulders. Some had their hair tied up with a feather that stuck up at a slant. Another had a fox tail hanging out of his hair. These Indians left their bows and arrows a quarter of a mile from town as they had been told to do. They were given fitting entertainment, and they ate liberally of the English food. They seemed to be friendly. They sang and danced in their manner.

One had something like a bow case about his waist filled with corn meal. He mixed a little with water and they ate some. He also had tobacco, but the others only smoked when he said so. Some of them had their faces painted black from forehead to chin, four or five fingers broad. Others had their faces painted in other fashions.

The Indians brought the stolen tools with them and a few skins to trade. They were asked to bring more skins, and they said they would. Then they were dismissed as soon as possible. But Samoset said he was sick and stayed until Wednesday morning. Then he was sent away with a hat, a pair of stockings and shoes, a shirt, and a piece of cloth to tie about his waist.

[Squanto comes with Samoset to prepare a meeting with the great sachem Massasoit]

Thursday, the twenty-second of March, was a fair warm day. About noon the people met on public business. They had met scarcely an hour when Samoset came bringing with him Squanto, of whom he had spoken. They brought some few skins to trade, some red herrings, newly taken and dried, but not salted. They told that their great sachem Massasoit was near-by with his brother Quadequina and all their men.

The two Indians could not say very well in English what they wanted to, but after an hour the king came to the top of a hill just opposite. He had in his train sixty men. The two groups of men stood looking at each other. The men of the plantation were not willing to send their Governor and the Indians were unwilling to come. So Squanto went again to Massasoit, and brought back word that the English should send someone to parley with him. Edward Winslow was sent to know Massasoit's mind and let the Governor's mind and will be known, which was to have trade and peace.

They sent the king a pair of knives and a copper chain with a jewel in it. To his brother they sent a knife, a jewel to hang in his ear, a pot of brandy, a good quantity of biscuit, and some butter. All was willingly accepted.

Edward Winslow, the messenger, made this speech to Massasoit: that King James saluted him with words of love and peace, and did accept him as his friend and ally. The Governor desired to see him and trade with him, and confirm a peace with him as his next neighbor. Massasoit liked well the speech, and heard it with attention, although the interpreters did not well express it.

After Massasoit had eaten and drunk himself, and given the rest to his company, he looked at Winslow's sword and armor. He showed his desire to buy it, but Winslow showed his unwillingness to part with it. In the end he left Winslow in the custody of Quadequina and came over the brook with

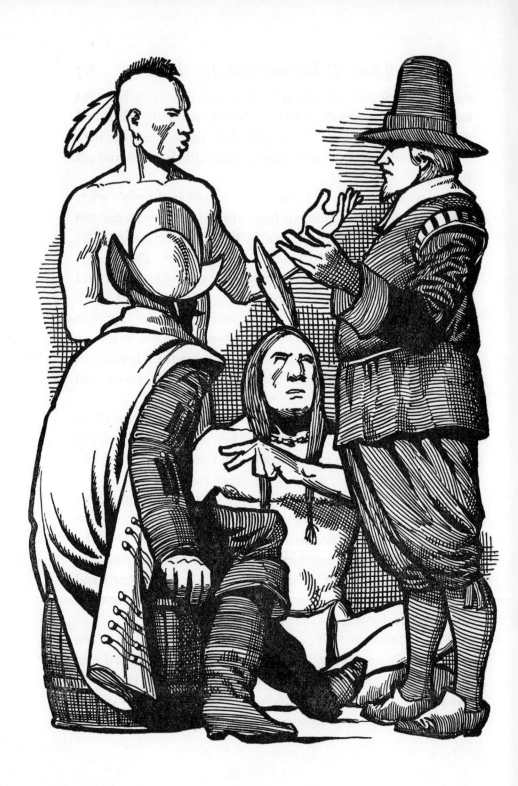

twenty men following him, leaving their bows and arrows behind. The English kept six or seven as hostages for Winslow.

[The Governor sits down with Massasoit and
a peace treaty is made]

Captain Standish and Mr. Allerton met the king at the brook with half a dozen musketeers. They saluted him and he them. A man on either side, they conducted him to a house being built where a green rug and three or four cushions were placed. Then instantly came the Governor, a drum and trumpet after him, and some musketeers. After salutations, the Governor kissed Massasoit's hand and the king kissed the Governor. Then they sat down. The Governor called for brandy and drank to Massasoit. Massasoit drank a great draught, that made him sweat all the while after. Governor Carver called for a little fresh meat. The king ate willingly and gave his followers some. Then they treated of peace. Here are the terms:

1. That neither Massasoit nor any of his men should injure or do hurt to any of the people of Plymouth.

2. That if any of the Indians did hurt to any of the men of the plantation, the offender should be sent for punishment.

3. If anything were taken away of theirs, Massasoit should cause it to be restored, and they would do the same for anything of his.

4. If anyone unjustly warred against Massasoit, they should aid him. If any warred against them, he should come to their aid.

5. He should send word of the peace to his confederate Indian neighbors and allies, so they would not attack or

wrong the men of the plantation, but might be included in the conditions of peace.

6. That when the Indians came, they should leave their bows and arrows behind them.

In his person, Massasoit was a very lusty man, in his best years. He was of able body, grave, and spare of speech. He wore little or nothing different from the rest of his followers, except for a great chain of white bone beads around his neck. Behind his neck hung a little bag of tobacco. He took some out to smoke and offered his pipe around. His face was painted deep red, a sort of mulberry. His head and face were oiled and glistened. All his followers likewise had their faces painted, in part or in whole. Some were black, some red, some yellow, and some white. They were painted with crosses or other patterns. Some wore skins and some were almost naked. They were all strong tall men. Massasoit had a great long knife hanging from a string around his neck. He marveled much at the trumpet and had it sounded for him many times.

So, after all was done, the Governor conducted Massasoit to the brook. They embraced and he departed. The hostages were kept while Winslow's return was awaited. But word was brought that Quadequina was coming. He was taken to the house Massasoit had been taken to. He was fearful of the muskets and made signs of dislike, so they were removed. He was a tall young man of very modest and pleasing appearance. They entertained him and he seemed to enjoy it. When he left, Winslow returned and the hostages were allowed to leave. Massasoit then returned to his place called Sowams, some forty miles away.

[Squanto stays, they learn of his capture and
escape to England]

Squanto stayed with them and was their interpreter. He
was a special instrument sent of God for their good and beyond their expectation. He showed them how to plant
their corn, where to fish and get other things, and was also
their pilot to bring them to unknown places for their profit,
and never left them till he died.

Squanto had been carried away from Patuxet with several others by a man named Hunt, master of a ship. Hunt
meant to sell them for slaves in Spain, but Squanto got
away to England, where he was taken in by a merchant of
London. He was used on voyages to Newfoundland and
other places, and finally brought here by a Mr. Dermer,
who came to these parts for discovery and other designs.

[They learn an English trader had troubles
with the Indians here]

I should say something about Mr. Dermer because it is
mentioned in a book published in 1622 by the President and
Council for New England that he made peace between the
savages of these parts and the English. It is said that this
plantation had the benefit of this peace. What a peace it was
is clear from what happened to him and his men. This Mr.
Dermer was here the same year the *Mayflower* came. An
account written by him bears the date June 30, 1620, so he
was in this very place only four months earlier. He writes
the following:

I will first begin with that place from which Squanto was
taken away. On Captain Smith's map it is called Plymouth.
I would like the first plantation seated here if there are

as many as fifty people or more. Otherwise at Charlton [Charlestown] because the savages are less to be feared there. The Pocanockets west of Plymouth bear much malice to the English and are stronger than all the savages from there to Penobscot.

Their desire for revenge was caused by an Englishman. Having them on board, he made a great slaughter with his shot-filled cannon, when (they say) they offered no injury on their part. Whether they were English or not is doubtful, yet the Indians believe so, partly because they listen to the French so much. Squanto cannot deny but they would have killed me when I was at Namasket had he not pleaded for me so hard.

The soil of the border of this great bay may be compared to most of the plantations I have seen in Virginia. The land is of various sorts. Patuxet has a hardy but strong soil. Nauset and Satucket are for the most part a deep mold, much like that where the best tobacco grows in Virginia. In the bottom of the great bay is store of cod and bass or mullet and other fish. But above all, Pocanocket has the richest soil and much open ground for English grain.

Massachusetts is about nine leagues from Plymouth and the waters between are full of islands and peninsulas which are very fertile for the most part.

Mr. Dermer was taken prisoner by the Indians at Manamoyick, a place not far from here and now well known. He gave them what they demanded for his liberty, but when they had got what they wanted, they kept him still and tried to kill his men. But he was freed by seizing some of them and keeping them bound till they gave him a canoe load of corn.

Afterward he came to the Isle of Capawack and Squanto with him. Going ashore among the Indians to trade as he usually did, he was betrayed and attacked. All his men were slain except the one who watched the boat. He got aboard very sorely wounded, and they would have cut off his head on the cuddy of his boat had not the man rescued him with a sword. They got away and managed to get to Virginia, where he died. Whether he died of his wounds or diseases of the country is uncertain. By all this it may appear how far these people were from peace, and with what danger this plantation was begun, save as the powerful hand of the Lord did protect them.

These things were partly the reason why the Indians kept apart and were so long before they came to the people of the plantation. Another reason (as the Indians themselves told later) was that three years earlier a French ship was cast away at Cape Cod. The men got ashore and saved their lives and much of their food and other goods. After the Indians heard of it, they gathered together from these parts, and kept a watch on them till they got the advantage, and killed all but three or four. They kept them and sent them from one sachem to another, to make sport with, and used them worse than slaves. Mr. Dermer redeemed two of them, and the Indians thought the *Mayflower* had come to get revenge.

Also, before they came to the English to make friendship, they got all the powwows of the country for a three-day assembly and service in a dark and dismal swamp to curse and cast spells in a horrid and devilish manner.

CHAPTER XIII

Of the Mayflower's Departure and the Planting of Corn

THEY made ready to send the *Mayflower* back at the beginning of April. The reason she stayed so long was the necessity and danger that lay upon them. It was well toward the end of December before she could land anything, or they able to receive anything ashore. Then later, on the fourteenth of January the common house they had made for a general gathering place caught fire and burned. Some had to return on shipboard for shelter. Then the sickness hit them hard and slowed their work. The Governor and the leaders, seeing so many die and fall sick daily, thought it not wise to send the ship away. With their condition and the danger from the Indians, they must first have some shelter. They thought it better to add costs on themselves and their friends at home than to risk all.

The master and the seamen, though before they hurried the passengers ashore to be gone, now changed. Many of their men being dead, and the ablest and many of the rest sick and weak, the master dare not put to sea till he saw his men begin to recover, and the heart of winter over.

Afterward as many as were able began to plant corn. Squanto was of great help. He showed them how to set it in the ground and how to tend it when it came up. Also he told them if they did not put a fish in the ground with the seed for fertilizer, in these long-used fields it would come to nothing. He told them that in the middle of April enough fish would come up the brook, and he showed them how to catch them. He showed them where to get other necessary things, all of which they found true by trial and experience. They sowed some English seed, wheat and peas, which came to no good, either because of the badness of the seed or lateness of the season, or both, or something else.

[Governor Carver dies and William Bradford
is elected in his place]

In the month of April while they were busy about their seed, their Governor, Mr. John Carver, came out of the field very sick on a hot day. He complained greatly of his head and lay down. Within a few hours his senses failed,

and he never spoke again before he died a few days later. His death was much lamented and caused great heaviness of heart among them. He was buried in the best manner possible, with some volleys of shot by all that bore arms. His wife, being a weak woman, died five or six days after him.

Shortly after, William Bradford was chosen Governor in his place. Bradford, not being yet recovered from his illness, from which he nearly died, Isaac Allerton was chosen to be his assistant. Bradford continued as Governor some years by renewed election every year, which I here note once for all.

CHAPTER XIV

Of a Visit to Massasoit and Adventures on the Way

HAVING in some sort ordered their business at home, it was thought a good thing to send some men out to see their new friend Massasoit. They would give him some gift to bind him faster to them in friendship. Also, they wanted to agree to some rules about the near-by Indians visiting so much and getting in the way, and satisfy some claims of injury the Indians made against the people of Plymouth. If they got the chance, they might view the country and see how Massasoit lived, what strength he had, and study the trails.

For these and the like ends, the Governor chose Stephen Hopkins and Edward Winslow to go, with Squanto for guide and interpreter. A horseman's coat of red cotton with an edging of lace, along with some lesser gifts, was sent to Massasoit to make them and their message more welcome.

They set forward the second of July about nine o'clock in the morning. Squanto was set on resting that night at Namasket, a town under Massasoit. Hopkins and Winslow thought the town must be very near because its people flocked so thick amongst them in Plymouth on the slightest occasion, but they found it was fifteen miles. On the way they found some ten or twelve men, women and children who had pestered them in Plymouth till they were weary of them. As the manner of all the Indians is, they go where food is easiest to get, especially in summer. As the bay at Plymouth afforded many lobsters, they came there every spring tide. Now they returned to Namasket with Winslow and Hopkins.

They went there about three o'clock in the afternoon. The people entertained them with joy, in the best way they could. They gave them bread made of corn and the spawn of shad which they had in great abundance. With the spawn they boiled musty acorns. Winslow and Hopkins ate heartily of the spawn and left the acorns. After this they desired one of them to shoot at a crow, complaining what damage it did to the corn. They shot and killed it at some four score yards, which the Indians much admired.

Squanto then said they would hardly reach Pocanocket in one day, saying they should go eight miles farther, where they would find better food. Being willing to hasten the journey, Winslow and Hopkins set out with him. Reaching a river at sunset, they found some of the Namaskets fishing upon a weir, where they caught an abundance of bass. The Indians welcomed them and gave them fish, and they gave the Indians some of their food, not doubting that they should have enough wherever they went. They slept in the open fields, for the Indians had no houses, though they spent most of the summer there.

The river had many towns on it, being of a good length. Thousands of men had lived along it, but most of them had died in the recent plague. They thought it a pity to see so many goodly fields, and so well-seated, lying idle and uncared for. Upon this same river dwelt Massasoit.

Next morning they broke fast and took their leave. Six savages went with them. They went six miles beside the river until they came to a shallow place. The Indians told them to take off their breeches, for they must wade through.

Here should be told of the valor and courage of some of the savages on the opposite side of the river. Only two men remained alive, both of them old. Seeing a company of men entering the river, these two ran very swiftly and low in the grass, to meet them at the bank. With shrill voices and great courage they charged upon the men in the river with their bows, asking who they were. They supposed the newcomers to be enemies and thought to take advantage of them in the water. But seeing they were friends, the old men welcomed them with such food as they had, and they were given a small bracelet of beads.

Having refreshed themselves, they continued their journey. The weather was very hot for travel, yet the country was so well watered that a man could scarce be dry. He would always have a spring at hand to cool his thirst, and plenty of small rivers besides. The Indians would only drink from a spring head.

When they came to a small brook with no bridge, the Indians offered to carry them across to keep them dry. Fearing Winslow and Hopkins would get weary, they offered to carry their muskets. Or if they wanted to remove some of their clothing, they would carry it. As they found more special kindness from Winslow or Hopkins, they would offer help to that one.

Much of the land along the way was cleared for cultivation, although now the weeds grew higher than their heads. They saw much good timber: oak, walnut, fir, beech, and exceedingly great chestnut trees. Then they came to another town of Massasoit's, where they ate oysters and fish.

[They arrive at Sowams and meet with Massasoit]

From there they went to Sowams, but Massasoit was not at home. They waited while Massasoit was sent for. When they heard he was coming, Squanto asked that their pieces be fired as a salute at their meeting. But when one of them started to load, the women and children were afraid and ran away. They could not be pacified until he put his musket down and Squanto explained.

Massasoit came and they fired a salute. He, in his manner, kindly welcomed them. He took them into his house and had them sit down by him. Winslow and Hopkins delivered the message and gave him the presents. Massasoit put on the red coat and a chain around his neck. He was not a little proud to see himself, and his men also to see their king so bravely dressed.

For answer to the message, he told them they were welcome and he would gladly continue the peace and friendship that was between them. As for his men, they should no more pester the people of the plantation as they had done. He would help them get corn for seed as they had asked.

This being done, his men gathered near him, and he began a speech. The men broke in to confirm what he said and to applaud. The meaning seemed to be, as far as they could learn, something like this: Was not he, Massasoit, commander of the country about them? Was not this town his, and the people of it? And should he not bring his skins to Patuxet to trade with them? Was not such and such a place his? He named at least thirty, and his men agreed and applauded each one. It was all very delightful, but tedious after a while.

Being ended at last, he lighted a pipe of tobacco and passed it around. He fell to talking of our king's majesty.

Also he talked of the French, bidding us not to suffer them to come to Narragansett Bay, for it was King James's country and he was King James's man.

It grew late, but he offered no food. Indeed, he had none, being so newly come home. So they desired to go to rest. He had Winslow and Hopkins get on the bed with himself and his wife, they at the one end and Winslow and Hopkins at the other. The bed was only planks laid a foot off the ground with a thin mat on them. Two more of his chief men joined them on the bed and pressed upon them for want of room. They were worse weary of their lodging than of their journey.

The next day many of their sagamores (lesser chief men) came to see Winslow and Hopkins, and many of their men came too. They started their games. The winners got skins and knives. Winslow and Hopkins challenged them to a shooting contest for skins, but the Indians dared not. They did want to see a piece fired at a mark. Hail-shot was used, and the Indians wondered to see the mark so full of holes.

About one o'clock Massasoit brought two fish that he had shot with an arrow. They were like bream, but three times as big and better meat. These were boiled but there were at least forty people waiting to get a share of them. Most had some of them. This was the only meal in two nights and a day. And had not one of them brought a partridge, they would have made the journey home without food. The Indians used not to have as much corn as they have since the English supplied them with hoes and showed them how to break more ground.

Massasoit tried to persuade them to stay longer, but they wanted to keep the Sabbath at home. And they feared they might be lightheaded for want of sleep. What with bad lodging, the Indians' noisy singing (they sang themselves to

sleep every night), lice and fleas within doors and mos-
quitoes without, they could hardly sleep all the time they
were there. They feared if they stayed any longer, they
would lack the strength to get home.

[They return to Plymouth]

So on Friday morning, before sunrise, they took their
leave and departed. Massasoit was both grieved and
ashamed that he could not better entertain them. He kept
Squanto to send from place to place to get skins to trade to
the men of Plymouth. To take Squanto's place as guide, he
appointed Tokamahamon, who was always found faithful.

Winslow and Hopkins came home weary and hungry.
They reported Massasoit's place to be forty miles from
Plymouth. They told of the great sickness which fell in
these parts about three years before the coming of the English. So many died they were not able to bury them. They
reported skulls and bones in many places lying still above
ground where their houses had been. A very sad sight to behold. They brought word of the Narragansett Indians who
lived on the other side of the great bay and were a strong
people. They were many in number, living close together,
and had not at all been touched by the plague.

CHAPTER XV

Of a Lost Boy and His Being Found
by the Indians

ABOUT the end of July, young John Billington lost himself in the woods. He wandered up and down five days, living on berries and what he could find. At length he came on an Indian settlement twenty miles south of Plymouth called Manomet. The Indians took him farther off to Nauset, among those people that had attacked the English while their ship lay at the Cape, as told before.

The Governor had someone ask the Indians about Billington. Massasoit found out where he was and sent word. Ten men were sent in the shallop to Nauset. They set out in fair weather, but before they had been long at sea, a storm arose with wind and rain. There was much lightning and thunder, and a water spout arose not far from them. But God be praised, it did not last long. They put in that night for harbor at Cummaquid, where they had some hope to find the boy. They had Squanto and Tokamahamon with them.

As it was night before they came in, they anchored in the midst of the bay, where they were dry at low tide. In the morning, they saw the savages seeking lobsters. With the channel between them, they sent Squanto and Tokamahamon to talk with them. Squanto and Tokamahamon told them who they were and why they came. They told the Indians not to be afraid, for no harm would come to them.

Their answer was that the boy was well, but he was at Nauset. Yet since they were there, they desired the men of Plymouth to come ashore and eat with them. As soon as their boat floated, they did. They went six ashore, leaving four Indian hostages in the boat to make sure of their safety while ashore. They were brought to the sachem, called Iyanough. He was a man not more than twenty-six years of age and very personable, gentle, courteous, and fair-conditioned. Indeed, he was not like a savage at all except for what he wore. He entertained them fittingly.

One thing there was heart-breaking. There was an old woman who seemed a hundred years old. She came to see them because she had never seen the English. But she could not see them without breaking forth weeping and crying. They asked the reason of it and were told she had had three sons who went aboard Master Hunt's ship to trade and were carried captive to Spain (when Squanto was carried away). She was deprived of the comfort of her children in her old age. She was told how sorry they were that any Englishman should do such a thing and that Hunt was a bad man. All the English that heard of what he did condemned him for it, and they would not harm the Indians if it gave them all the skins in the country. She was given a small present, which quieted her.

After dinner they took boat for Nauset, Iyanough and two of his men coming along. The day and tide were almost spent before they came to Nauset. They could not get in with their shallop. Iyanough and his men went ashore. Squanto went to tell Aspinet, sachem of Nauset, what they came for. After sunset Aspinet came with a great train of

his people and brought the boy with him. One Indian carried him through the water. There were at least a hundred Indians. Half of them came to the shallop's side unarmed, the others stood back with their bows and arrows. Aspinet gave them the boy all hung with beads and made his peace. They gave Aspinet a knife and another to the Indian who first took care of John Billington and brought him to Nauset. Then the Indians left. Later they came and made their peace, and were repaid for their corn that had been taken when the *Mayflower* first came to the Cape the year before.

Hearing report of Indian trouble at home, they hastened away, as the colony was weakly guarded. But the wind was contrary. Having little fresh water left and being sixteen leagues from home, they put in to shore. Iyanough met them again and the most of his town. He was still willing to help them. Taking a small barrel, he led some of the men a great way in the dark for water, but could find none that was good. He brought them what he could find. Meanwhile, the women joined hand in hand, singing and dancing before the shallop. The men showed all the kindness they could. Iyanough himself took a bracelet from about his neck and hung it on one of the English. By God's providence they came safely home and found the alarm false.

Thus peace and acquaintance was pretty well established with the natives about them. Another Indian called Hobomok came to live with them. He was a lusty man known for his valor and bearing amongst the Indians. Hobomok was very faithful and loyal to the English till he died.

CHAPTER XVI

Of Squanto's Capture and a Show of Strength Among the Indians

HOBOMOK and Squanto went on some business among the Indians. When they were returning, near the Indian town of Namasket, fourteen miles west of Plymouth, they met a sagamore called Corbitant. He was allied to Massasoit, but no friend to the English to this day. Whether it was out of envy of them or hatred of the English, he began to quarrel with them and tried to stab Hobomok. Hobomok, being quick and strong, broke away and came running, all covered with sweat, and told the Governor what had happened. He feared Squanto had been killed. The Governor, taking counsel, saw this could not be tolerated. If they should allow their friends and messengers to be wronged, none would stand by them or tell them anything important, or do anything for them. Next, they might even join the attackers.

It was decided to send Captain Standish and ten well-armed men to attack the Indians by night. If they found Squanto was killed, they were to cut off Corbitant's head, but not to hurt any but those who had a hand in it. Hobomok was asked if he would go and be their guide, and bring them there before daybreak. He said he would, and bring them to the house where Corbitant lay, and show them which was he.

So they set forth the fourteenth of August and surrounded the house. The Captain, giving charge to let none pass out, entered the house to search for Corbitant. But he was gone away that day, so they missed him. They found that Squanto was alive and that Corbitant had only threatened to kill him, making a move to stab him, but not doing it. So they withheld and did no more hurt. The people came trembling and brought the best food they had after Hobomok told what was intended.

Three who broke out of the house were sorely wounded when they tried to pass the guard. These Captain Standish brought home with them, where their wounds were dressed and cured, and then they were sent home. After this they had many congratulations from different sachems, and much firmer peace. Even the Indians of the Isle of Capawack sent to make friendship. And this Corbitant himself used Massasoit as a go-between to make his peace, but shied away from them for a long while after.

After this, it seemed good to the company in general that though they had been threatened by the Indians of Massachusetts, they should go amongst them. They went partly to see the country, partly to make peace with them, and partly to trade.

[They go to Massachusetts Bay
to meet the Indians there and trade]

The Governor chose ten men fit for the purpose, with Squanto and two other Indians to interpret. They set out on Tuesday, the eighteenth of September, about midnight, when the tide was right. They supposed Massachusetts Bay to be nearer. It turned out to be about twenty leagues from

New Plymouth. They came to the bottom of the Bay late on Wednesday, anchored and stayed in the shallop that night without seeing any Indians.

The next morning they put in to shore. There they found many lobsters that had been gathered by the Indians. They built a fire and cooked them beside a cliff. Then Captain Standish set two sentinels behind the cliff to landward to guard the shallop. He took four men and Squanto as guide and set out to find some Indians. They met a woman coming for her lobsters. They told her about eating them and paid her for them. She told where the people were. Squanto went to the Indians while Miles Standish and the four men came back to the shallop with directions which way to go.

The sachem was Obbatinewat, and though he lived at the bottom of Massachusetts Bay, he was under Massasoit's rule. He treated them very kindly. He said he dared not stay in one place because of the raids of the Tarentines from the northeast coast, who came in the harvest time to take away their corn and kill them. He said the Squaw Sachem or Queen of the Massachusetts was an enemy to him, but they asked him to take them to her anyway.

[They search for the Squaw Sachem]

They crossed the bay, which was very large with at least fifty islands in it. The Indians were not sure how many islands there were. It was night before they got across the bay. The Indians went on shore, but found nobody. That night they rode at anchor in the shallop.

The next day, Friday, the twenty-first of September, they went ashore and marched into the country. After about three miles, they came to a place where corn had been newly gathered, a house pulled down, and the people gone. A mile from there Nanepashemet, their king, had lived

before his death. His house was not like others, but was on top of a large scaffold built with poles and planks, some six feet from the ground, and on a hilltop.

Not far from this, in a low place, they came to a fort built by the dead king. It was built of poles thirty or forty feet long set closely together. They enclosed a ring about fifty feet across. A breast high trench was dug on both sides. The only entrance was over a bridge. In the middle of the palisade stood the frame of a house where the king lay buried. A mile from there was another fort on top of a hill, deserted since the king's death.

They stayed here and sent out two Indians to look for the people and to tell them of their visitors. About a mile away the two Indians found the women of the place huddled together with their corn in heaps. They had fled there out of fear of Miles Standish and his men.

At first the Indian women entertained them out of fear, but seeing how gently they were treated, they took heart and became more friendly. They boiled cod and cooked such other things as they had. At length, with much sending for, one of their men came, trembling with fear. When he saw no hurt was intended, he promised to trade his beaver skins with them. He was asked about their queen, but it seemed she was far away. At least they did not get to see her.

[They finish trading and return to Plymouth]

Squanto would have had them take the skins away from the women. He said, "They are a bad people and have often threatened you."

But he was told, "Were they never so bad, we would not wrong them, or give them any just occasion against us. For their words, we little weigh them, but if they once attempt anything against us, we will deal with them far worse than you propose."

Having spent a good part of the day, they returned to the shallop, with almost all the women coming to trade. The women sold the coats off their backs. They tied boughs about them, for they were more modest than some English women are. They promised the Indians to come again, and the Indians promised for their part to save their beaver skins to trade.

The Indians said there were two rivers that came into the bay, but there was no time to explore them. The harbors were the best in the world for shipping, and at the entrance of the bay were many rocks that looked like very good fishing grounds. The islands had all been cleared for crops, but the people were all dead or gone. Their food growing scarce, the wind coming fair, and having moonlight, they set out that evening. Through the goodness of God they came safely home before noon next day. They made report of the place, wishing they had settled there. But the Lord, who gives all men the bounds of their living place, had set it aside for other use. And thus they found the Lord to be with them in all their ways, and to bless their outgoings and incomings, for which let His Holy Name have praise forever, to all posterity.

CHAPTER XVII

Of Their Thanksgiving

THEY began now to gather in the small harvest they had, and to fit up their houses and dwellings against winter. All were well recovered in health and strength, and had all things in good plenty. For while some were busy with exploring and trading or Indian matters, others were fishing for cod, bass, and other fish. They took good store and every family had its portion. All summer there was no want. And now began to come plenty of fowl as winter approached. Fowl had been abundant when they first came, but afterward decreased by degrees. Besides waterfowl, there was great store of wild turkeys, of which they took many, venison, and other game. They had about a peck of meal a week for each person, or now since harvest, that amount of Indian corn. All of this made many afterward write so largely of their plenty here to their friends in Enggland. What they said was not made up, but true reports.

The harvest gotten in, the Governor sent four men out fowling, so they could rejoice together after they had gathered the fruits of their labor. The four in one day killed enough fowl to feed the whole company a week with a few other things added. As a part of their recreations they had shooting matches.

Many of the Indians came amongst them. Among the rest was Massasoit with some ninety men. They were entertained and feasted for three days. The Indians went out and killed five deer, which they brought to the plantation and gave to the Governor, the Captain, and others. And although it be not always so plentiful as it was at this time, yet by the goodness of God the plantation was so far from want that they often wished those in England and Holland sharers of the plenty.

Thus out of small beginnings greater things have been produced by His hand that made all things of nothing, and gives being to all things that are. And as one small candle may light a thousand, so the light here kindled hath shone to many, yea in some sort to our whole nation. Let the glorious name of Jehovah have all the praise.

I have written this account that the children may see with what difficulties their fathers wrestled in going through these things in their first beginnings, and how God brought them along notwithstanding all their weaknesses and infirmities. Also that some use may be made hereof in after times, by others in such like weighty employments.

Psalm 100

Make a joyful noise unto the LORD, all ye lands.

Serve the LORD with gladness: come before his presence with singing.

Know ye that the LORD he is God: it is he that hath made us, and not we ourselves; we are his people, and the sheep of his pasture.

Enter into his gates with thanksgiving, and into his courts with praise: be thankful unto him, and bless his name.

For the LORD is good; his mercy is everlasting; and his truth endureth to all generations.

NOTE: This text is from the King James Version of the Bible. Probably the Geneva Bible was used for church services; however, copies of the King James Version were in the homes of some of the Colonists. Psalm 100 in the King James Version seems more appropriate to the celebration of a Thanksgiving than the version in the Geneva Bible. For church singing the *Ainsworth Psalter* was used. In it the psalms are rhymed and arranged to fit the tune. The tune for Psalm 100 is commonly known as "Old Hundred."

A Word About the Text

THE AUTHORS have adapted and selected from the original texts to highlight the dramatic narrative while preserving historical accuracy. William Bradford's history, *Of Plimoth Plantation,* is used exclusively until the arrival of the *Mayflower* at Cape Cod, then the journals of Bradford and Edward Winslow, known as *Mourt's Relation,* which Bradford used in writing his history, are brought into the account to give the first-freshness and immediacy of their experience. Bradford left out some colorful detail to give distance and dignity to his history. Of course he adds much that is good also. Although early seventeenth-century syntax has been untangled, pronoun antecedents made more exact, and archaic words modernized, an attempt has been made to preserve the flavor of Bradford's language and the spirit of the times. Religious controversy has been left out, but the devotional tone kept. Dates used are Old Style, ten days behind the New Style (modern) calendar. The texts used are:

Bradford, William. *Of Plimoth Plantation*. Commonwealth Edition, Boston, 1898.

Arber, Edward. *The Story of the Pilgrim Fathers* (containing the text of *Mourt's Relation*). London, 1897.

Acknowledgments

Acknowledgment is made to:

The scholarship of Samuel Eliot Morison.

The scholarship of Edward Arber.

Waldo Heinrichs for historical advice and editing.

David B. Freeman, Director of Plimoth Plantation, and Arthur G. Pyle, Director of Education of Plimoth Plantation, for review and suggestions.

Elizabeth W. Smith and Mary M. Meredith for careful reading of the manuscript and suggestions.

Main Historical Persons

Samoset   Sagamore of a tribe located in what is now Maine. He was left on the shore of Cape Cod by an English trader shortly before the Pilgrims landed. He walked into Plymouth in the early spring of 1621.

Squanto   A member of the tribe that had lived at Patuxet, the Indian name for Plymouth. He was believed to be the only survivor of a plague that wiped out the village in 1617. He was captured by a trader who meant to sell him as a slave in Spain, but he escaped to England, where he lived awhile. He returned to New England and came to Cape Cod with a Mr. Dermer. Squanto stayed with the colony at Plymouth after he was brought there by Samoset.

Hobomok   A Wampanoag Indian who came to live with the Pilgrims and help them as Squanto did.

Corbitant   Sagamore of the neighboring Pocasset Indians who threatened to kill Squanto and Hobomok on one of their journeys.

Glossary of Words with
Older and Special Meanings

compact An agreement between two or more people, states, groups, parties.

congregation A gathering of people or things, a religious assembly.

covenant A compact, a binding and solemn agreement, an agreement among members of a church to hold to points of doctrine, faith, etc.

furnish In its older meaning, to supply, equip, a horse would be furnished with horse furniture — saddle, bridle, etc.

harry To torment, harass, to raid and destroy, plunder.

lusty In the older meaning, full of life, manly, strong.

matchlock A gunlock fired by touching a burning wick or cord to the powder charge, a musket so fired.

palisade A row of large pointed stakes set in the ground to make a fence around a fort.

parley To have a talk or discussion, especially with an enemy.

patent A document open to public examination and granting a certain right, as to settle in a particular place.

piece An older term for any firearm, still used by soldiers.

plantation A place where a colony is settled, or planted.

powwow   Indian medicine man or priest.

sachem   An important Indian chief, usually, sometimes same as sagamore.

sagamore   A lesser Indian chief.

shallop   An open boat fitted with oars or sails or both; the shallop on the *Mayflower* had both and was large enough to hold thirty or forty men.

squibs   Homemade firecrackers.

strangers   Pilgrim term for those people who had not been members of the Leyden church; they were recruited by the merchants in England. Some did not fit in very well; others, like Miles Standish and John Alden, did.

Index